MY COMPUTER TALKS A WHOLE NEW LANGUAGE. HELP!

This book is for your general interest. None of its contents or comments should be acted upon without considering your own circumstances and any risks involved, and if need be seeking professional advice. Act always with caution in matters of computer and internet security. Information has been provided in good faith. Statements about technical fact or nomenclature may differ from what professional computer experts might agree with. This arrangement and design ©2010 Will Smyth

WILL SMYTH

MY COMPUTER TALKS A WHOLE NEW LANGUAGE.
HELP!

AN UN-GEEKY COMPUTER WORDLIST

More than 200 selected words

including many Internet terms

aHansel^{imprint}

It is not the strongest of the species that survive, nor the most intelligent, but the one most responsive to change.
Charles Darwin (1809 –1882)

(hmm ... I wonder if computers are here to stay ☺)

COMPUTERS RULE. RIGHT?

There exist heaps of computer dictionaries. They'd make a really *big* heap for a bonfire!

But heck, we're not fans of book burning.

A funny thing is that some people thought the coming of computers would mean books and print would hardly be around any more. We'd have "the paperless society," clear desks at the office—yeah, right—and never read a book.

But that did not happen. Maybe it was the same people, or their moms and dads, who once reckoned that television would completely kill off big-screen movies.

Well, movies survived, and books too—even dictionaries.

This book is more than a simple word-list and less than a heavy-duty batch of techno-babble. The writer is a simple-minded senior who wondered what it all meant, and what went where, when he bravely unwrapped a box with a computer inside.

The good news is that, as computers get smarter, they are more user-friendly. Nearly like in the movies: you get up, brush your teeth, then ask aloud, "Good morning, Hal. What's on the schedule for today?" Uh, bad example. If the computer in that movie was honest, it'd have to reply, "Well, first I'm going to mess with the spacecraft, then try to kill you" (in Stan Kubrick's *2001 A Space Odyssey*). That was in 1968. Computers were science fiction. Now we got 'em!

I was amused to look through the 1977 edition of the *Penguin Dictionary of Computers*. It had THREE THOUSAND entries of words and phrases, and fifty of the entries were long articles, on topics like "storage devices," "input devices," and "critical path method." Interestingly, that dictionary's first edition back in 1970 insisted that its purpose was to put difficult computer-speak into *everyday English*.

In 1993 along came the more readable *The Complete Idiot's Guide to Computer Terms*. Whereas the old-style dictionary from the '70s talked about punch-cards being fed into a computer from hoppers, the more relaxed 1990s book – with that kinda cool name – was happy to tell readers that *morphing* is a computer-aided special graphics effect where an image can be made to melt into another image, helpfully adding *"remember the villain in the film Terminator2?"* That guide, or dictionary, still had well over ONE THOUSAND entries.

Its more recent editions, by the way, are highly recommended, plus there are also plenty of technical reference works for specialists – they would scare away normal mortals, and are not needed by us – but at least their authors don't call us idiots and dummies.

What many of us *are*, are adults who did not grow up with computers and were nervous about starting an acquaintance, and had little motivation to try. We've heard some of the words in use. Webcam? Is it a kind of duck? Modem? Something to do with hair coloring? Fashion anyway. Our peers show us photos of the grandchilden, received as email attachments; they even get sent *videos* via their computer, for heaven's sake.

And you very probably know a down-home family somewhere who are developing a home business based on computer use – maybe marketing physical goods, or promoting various products and being paid commissions as 'affiliates' (see the third page of the word listings).

This short book has just over 200 entries. I avoided the technical stuff or it's out of my depth; and we're not worrying about the wider vocabulary of specialized areas such as online role-play gaming, or Internet Marketing (IM). Several mentions *do* come from those bodies of words. You will find for example *avatar* in the online game sense. Or, from marketing lingo, a few company names (*eBay, Clickbank, PayPal*) or products (e.g. *Camtasia,* for video home-studio software sold by TechSmith) and terms like *opt-in* and *login,* with or without the hyphens that start to disappear as new compounds and hybrid words gain favor.

That previous paragraph used the word *online* twice (no hyphen). This reflects two facts: (1) Computers are now increasingly likely to be connected to the Internet. So, that makes their activity "on-line". (2) And because we have gotten used to the word, we can drop the hyphen. But keep it if you want. Computer lingo is in a state of flux, as is language generally. The words of electronic technology arrive among us – and also change – faster than words about older traditional activities. Let's call it e-lingo and see if *that* term catches on!

I hope this helps you feel at home with your friendly computer. Our un-geeky book contains handy words that you will meet after you've brushed your teeth and told a shipboard computer (if you happen to be in a spaceship) to behave itself and not kill *anybody*.

Will

P.S. It soon becomes clear to the reader – and this is a book to *read* more than to consult – that my background is not technical. It is non-geeky. I fall back on the late Douglas Adams' famous work **The Hitch-Hiker's Guide to the Galaxy**, where we are told that the Guide itself (the one used by space travellers) **"although wildly inaccurate"**, scored by having the words **Don't Panic** in large friendly letters on the cover. Here they're quite tiny, and only on the back cover.

Words in italics have a separate entry in the word list. For example, in the very first entry below, you'll see the terms *URL*, *browser bar*, *on-line*, and *copy and paste*. Each has its own later entry.

A

active link If someone supplies you with an internet address (that is, a *URL*), perhaps scribbled on a piece of paper, you can go and type it carefully into the *browser bar*. In practise, at least when you are *on-line* (connected to the internet) you seldom do the typing. Instead, you either *copy and paste* the address into the browser bar, OR simply click your mouse pointer on the shown address which would look something like this – http://www.some-domain.com Then, if it takes you to the website in question, it was an **active link.**

active window The active 'window' is the part of the screen you are currently working in, as used by both the Apple Mac and the more common PC once referred to as "IBM-compatible" desktop or micro computers. Word-processing programs, for typing documents etc., use "pull-down windows" for the user's convenience. A great benefit is that you can have several windows open at the same time, but only one can be active at any one time. It is easy to switch between them, and then return to the one you were working on before – or to a different one. Each open window is the visible indication of a program that is running.

Adobe The word itself is 4000 years old and refers to a traditional building material of mud and straw (or similar) to make bricks. In the computer world it is the handy label for Adobe Systems Inc, a company which has well-known graphics programs on the market, and some are provided free for the end-user (you). So, your new computer may come with a pre-installed Adobe Acrobat program that lets the computer open and read documents called *PDF* files. Sometimes you will want to open that kind of file.

Adobe Illustrator is a drawing software by Adobe Inc.

Adobe Photoshop is another popular program by the Adobe company and as the name might suggest, it's for manipulating photographic images. It is one kind of *graphics editing* software.

ad An abbreviation of the word advertisement, as elsewhere in normal language use. Advertising revenue drives e-commerce, just as much as actual sales, whether of physical goods, or of services, or electronically delivered products (e.g. e-books and software).

add-in and **add-on** Yes, but what is added in-or-on to what? An **add-in** is any new software feature subsequently integrated with an existing computer program. The new feature (the add-in) can come as a product sold by a third party. One example: MSWord is the common word-processor program (and your computer probably has it installed), while, for writers and editors, one useful add-in to MSWord is the FileCleaner software. An **add-on** is similar except that it is not integrated with the original; merely – as the term add-on might suggest – an extra feature associated with the original one.

The Wikipedia online encyclopedia helpfully notes, "Add-on is often considered the general term comprising snap-ins, plug-ins, extensions, and themes."(!) That's nice. Neither you nor I needs to worry right now what any of **those** are. Phew.

affiliate   Many firms that sell their products *online* allow you to sign up as an "affiliate" and they pay a commission for each buyer sent to them. A good many individuals make a full-time living as affiliates. They maintain their own websites devoted to promoting (advertising) other people's products. It's called **affiliate marketing**, part of the overall *e-commerce* that is possible via a computer connected to the internet. Regarding such connections, see *internet service provider (ISP)*.

alphanumeric *characters* are the keyboard characters (a – z and 1234567890) letters of the alphabet and the numerals. The term excludes other characters – punctuation marks (!) or quite different symbols, for pictorial meanings (→▽), or just embellishment (ଔ ෴). A *Wikipedia* article notes that some alphanumeric sets, e.g. for coding electrical connections, omit items which might be confused: 0 zero with the letters O & Q; the numeral 1 with the lower case letter l (L); 2 with Z.

Alt   Alt is a shortening of the verb "to alternate", and on the keyboard it means "change (or switch) function." The Alt keys sit in the bottom row of the keyboard, one on either side of the space bar. It is worth looking at the article "alt key", on the *Wikipedia* online encyclopedia. In brief, some *shortcuts* happen when you press Alt plus one of the function keys in the top row, F1 thru F12. The MSWord 'Help' tool tells you more. There are two Alt keys for convenience of typing, same as there are two Shift keys – one each side – for making capital letters. However, with Mac computers the left and right Alt keys perform differently. Plenty of folk happily type for years without ever worrying about the mysterious Alt keys.

Android is the name of a series of smart-phones, hand-held phone/computer hybrids, web-connected, since late 2009.

anti-virus programs are proprietary security software programs to protect your computer from deliberate attack, mischievous invasion which some people think is amusing, no matter what harm and distress is caused to legitimate computer users. Use good and reputable anti-virus software.

AOL The letters came from America On Line, but AOL Inc, a Time Warner company, was "spun off" in December 2009 to become again a separate internet services company. The company has been best known for its "online software suite" which had a membership ("at its zenith", says *Wikipedia*) of thirty million members.

app short for application, commonly spoken by computer people who are too time-starved to say the whole word. Also found in computer magazines. An **application** is merely a software program, or a modification of a program, applied in a useful way and probably re-named to be a marketable e-commerce product.

Apple Inc and **Apple Mac** The **Mac**, or Macintosh, was the name given to a series of computers from the company **Apple Inc**. The Mac evolved from the Apple II and was the first commercially successful personal computer to use *mouse* and screen icons ("graphical user interface") instead of typed commands. The company was extremely successful until losing market share in the 1990s as the PC market moved in favor of machines running MS-DOS and MS Windows. However, Mac users typically love their Apple computers and the company has a 5% share of the world market which is a very large operation. The founders of Apple were *Steve Jobs*, Steve Wozniak, and Mike Markkula. Apple computers have their own distinct operating system, currently OS X version 10 "Snow Leopard". Macs with the Intel x86 chip *CPU* (central processing unit) can now even run the rival Microsoft

Windows system, but not vice-versa. Apple also make and market the *iPhone4* smart-phone device launched in 2010.

architecture is a term from its own profession, but computer geeks borrowed the word and in computer-speak it refers to the internal design, both physical and electronic, of *microprocessors*, *motherboards* and *towers*.

archive has its normal meanings, except that what is archived is either your own records, in *files* and *folders* (and see *housekeeping*), or else the computer's automatic systems for organizing programs and tracking when they were used, a procedure that need hardly concern the ordinary user.

arrow keys on your keyboard are for moving the cursor up, down, left and right. They move the cursor one space at a time as far as you choose, and without deleting anything on the way.

asterisk (*) Apart from its use in documents where you might want to type it as a regular character, the asterisk can be a *wild-card* symbol when you might be looking for a file and don't know the file's whole name. In that case you'd type the asterisk symbol * to represent the unknown piece. If you're a beginning user, no need to bother about this yet.

avatar   In certain online interactive games (role-play games) the players choose to "be" a character in the virtual world of the game. That's then the player's avatar, a kind of "other self" for the duration of the game – which might last for weeks or months. The avatar can be of a different sex from the player, or a different species if the world of the game permits this, like in fantasy role-play settings. ("My elf is smarter than your dwarf.")

auto-repeat Your keyboard probably has this feature. If you rest a finger a moment too long on any letter, or on the space bar, it might do thissssssssss or [this] before you notice. One of those little aids that is also a trap. ☺

auto-save Once upon a time, when we forgot to save work (Ctrl + s) we lost the work when we went for a cup of coffee and there was a power outage, or could be we closed the program forgetting we'd not saved. Cuss-words failed to recover the unsaved data. Computers got fed up with human frailty so now they just shrug and save the current work every few minutes. You're allowed to tell a computer how often you want it to save, and if you watch closely, you may see it smirk.

B

backup   We're always being told that it makes sense to back up files, especially files in folders of work we do, or just our personal documents and correspondence. I guess it's good advice. Back-up just means make a copy (which is easy with Word documents, in fact with any word processor program). You can even click to send a copy to be saved on an *external hard drive,* or to the *Server*'s computers. Some companies take big precautions against losing records, by backing up their data to computers located elsewhere, in case fire destroys the head office.

backspace   The backspace key will move the little winking *cursor* – yes, surprise, back one space, to the **left.** But doing so deletes whatever *character* was in the space. If you only want to move the cursor without any deletions, you use the *arrow keys*. If you use the actual delete key, it deletes the character to the **right**. Sounds awkward, but becomes second nature if you do a reasonable amount of simple typing.

beta   The beta version of a new software just means the trial version before it is released to the public (either for sale, or as part of a free-to-use service, for example by a public utility or government department). Typically a beta version will be trialled by some users who then say what they think of it, in return for the early access and perceived benefit that this offers.

Bing   Bing is the Microsoft company's search engine.

bitmap is a type of image-storing to which your computer gives the *file-extension* **.bmp**   Drawings usually are bitmaps.

blog Blog is an internet term which has entered the wider language. It started as short for "web log" meaning an individual's log (like a ship's log), a journal, on the *internet* or *web*. The "blogger" writes day-to-day diary notes on a personal *website*, mostly at first as straightforward text. In the last twenty years some blogging websites have become highly elaborate and not much different from corporate websites. They have ads, reviews, video, links, and comments posted by visitors (viewers). The big phenomenon of *social network sites* (Facebook, Twitter, Digg, Delicious), has grown from the blogging culture. There are free "hosted" blog sites, for example at Blogspot.com which is owned by Google, the largest company involved with internet business and advertising revenue.

bookmark, bookmarking Each *browser* allows the user to mark the webpage presently being visited as a "favorite" or as "bookmarked" making it easy to return to at a later date.

boot To boot or boot up your PC sounds cool e-lingo when you simply mean turning it on. Booting is not a term we users need to know about any longer, although it is not quite the same as just turning on the power switch. This hardly matters. You could think of it as kick-starting. Once, if your machine *crashed,* you needed some kind of re-boot floppy disc to coax it back to life. That's history. Current models have safe close-down systems and should get back on their own two feet.

broadband access or, high data-rate internet access. This is the faster kind of internet connection, as opposed to dial-up. For current internet use, a dial-up connection (of 56 kilobits per second) is seen as almost a liability rather than a functional tool. *Wikipedia* comment: "The trend is to raise the threshold of the broadband definition as the marketplace rolls out faster services."

browser   The browser is the program you employ to enter internet addresses (*URLs*) into the **browser bar**, which is the blank strip at top left of screen (when connected to internet). By default, a Windows-running computer will probably have as its browser Microsoft's Internet Explorer software. Another company offering a browser is Netscape. Other users prefer, say, the Firefox browser which is an *open-source software* developed by volunteers for Mozilla, owned by the not-for-profit Mozilla Foundation. It is fairly easy to switch between different browsers.

burning Not the same as *flaming.* Burning a disc means recording a CD or DVD on your own computer, either by copying an existing disc or by reading the digital information from, for instance, a *camcorder* that probably came with the software to do this. Companies that sell burning software offer products with names such as Ashampoo and Nero.

bus   This kind of bus is the cabled-together "highway" of wires for the computer's own internal communication. It's the B in *USB* for Universal Serial Bus, describing the kind of connection your computer's extra gadgets use.

C

calculator We once used small calculators in school, or watched them being operated by shopkeepers. You might not realize that the home computer has a calculator as a built-in feature. At the start-up (Welcome) screen, click on Start, then Programs, look for Accessories . . . and there it should be, in that pull-down list. Click on Calculator. It appears on your screen. Now you simply use it like a normal stand-alone calculator, except that you click on the buttons with your mouse pointer, not your finger. (Touch-sensitive screens now exist in some applications, including handheld devices.)

camcorder Sony made the branded Camcorder digital cameras or 'movie recorders'. The public seems to have embraced the name as the generic word for such devices. They have become smaller and very versatile, with easy connection (and software provided at purchase) for uploading both to the home computer and to *YouTube*. A typical camera of this kind now has a hard drive (no film, no tapes, no removable discs) and a dozen or more hours of "filming" time. If that isn't enough, they take still images too. Impressive.

Camtasia A computer product offered by the TechSmith company which allows a home-based user to make videos based on *screen capture* with added commentary or other audio. If used in conjunction with Microsoft's Vista or later operating system, Camtasia handles camcorder video too.

cancel Oftentimes the **cancel** button is the safe one you should hit (that is, click on). It means "I don't want to proceed with this." In effect this is the same as the *escape* action. It is NOT the same as *delete*, which does just that to what's highlighted on the screen. Clicking *cancel* will buy time to decide if you *really* want to do the other thing! See also *esc/escape*

Caps Lock   On the keyboard, left side above Shift. Tap once and you find that you're typing all in capitals, known as *upper case*. Tap again to restore to the normal letters, *lower case*. A tricky thing that catches people out (me!) is when you accidentally have Caps Lock on, and type in one of your *case-senitive* passwords, or so you fondly suppose. All your screen shows is a row of asterisks, and the wretched program refuses to accept your password. Yep. Caps Lock was on.

cascade   Not a waterfall. In the MSWord word processor, when there are several pull-down windows open, (for various programs) you can see them as overlapping panels, and that display is called a cascade.

case sensitive   means that it matters whether the text is in upper case (capital letters) or lower case (not capitals). An obvious time when it matters is when you are asked to give a password. Most passwords are case sensitive. From the computer's point of view, a letter and its corresponding capital are different *characters*.

C-drive etc. The computer's C-drive is normally the first or main hard-drive, perhaps the only one you ever use. The A-drive is for those little 3½ inch floppy discs. B-drive has become obsolete with disappearance of the 5¼ inch floppies. Your computer probably does have as a D-drive that in-and-out tray which can take a *CD-ROM* or a music CD or a movie DVD to play. If there's also a *disc burner* tray, your machine will label that as its E-drive. If you also have an external hard drive as an "optional extra", well, there's an F-drive. These labelings don't have to be the same for every computer, but that's how it goes.

CD-ROM This stands for Compact Disc Read-Only Memory. We just need to know that the computer "reads" info from it – instructions to run some program – but you can't mess with it or over-write it with other stuff. Why? Because it's Read-Only.

cell (in a spreadsheet) This kind of cell is the little box in which you can enter numerical data, in an accounting spreadsheet program such as Microsoft's Excel. The first vertical row of cells is called A, the second B... and so on. You can instruct the program to add the numbers in A and B and enter the new value in row C; and so on, down the column for all your collected data.

character This is not a shady character in a whodunnit book. A character is any letter, numeral or symbol that the keyboard has on it, AND many more that can be accessed from the computer's storage. For example, in the word processor MS Word you can find a serious number of different fonts (differently designed letters of the alphabet, in many sizes) plus at the bottom of the drop-down menu of fonts, several lots of *wingdings*, Windows' catchy name for a whole bunch of additional shapes. Also known as *dingbats*. Each is a character. There's the familiar smiley face ☺. There's a telephone ☏ and there are loads more. Also from the MS Word menu bar at the top, clicking Insert, then Symbol, you'd come across still more: the Euro money symbol € and Greek letters such as π "pi". One way or another, perhaps by downloading from specialist sites which provide them, you can get hold of just about any letter character from any language, including Russian, Hebrew, Chinese, Japanese, Hindi, Thai, or various Native North American scripts ... Cree, Inuit. And many more. What you want to *do* with them is up to you.

As you know, there are multiple variants of the "Latin" alphabet used by English. For example, we type c-a-f-e and the computer knows to give it the French acute accent over the letter e, like this...café. For other foreign words with exotic accents, or letters not used in English, we need to go find the right character from an appropriate *font* set..

chat rooms – a general term for "synchronous conferencing" where a registered member (a chatter) of a shared-interest group can exchange typed messages with fellow chatters in real time. *Yahoo* has a registry of currently available chat rooms. You could even start your own! There are other modes, but usually a chat room consists of a website to which potential members of an interest-group find their way. *Wikipedia* has a useful article. A search of the term **chat rooms** is likely to produce a first couple of pages of singles dating sites. The underwater basket-weaving fan club will be a few pages further on.

chip A computer chip is formally called a *microprocessor*. These are constantly being re-designed and manufactured for different computer requirements and client companies, just as diversely as the many models of cars we see on the road.

Clickbank Clickbank is a company which facilitates the selling of products by many thousands of vendors, in effect by being the seller and taking a commission. It is also the intermediary of choice for typical *affiliate marketers* who "drive traffic" (i.e. direct business prospects) to many of those vendors in return for their own share of commission revenue. Clickbank even gives a special name to the affiliates' user-names, calling them "nicks" (nicknames). This is one example of the jargon which accumulates around particular niches and sub-niches in the vast theater of the internet universe.

clipart Clip art – but written mostly as a single word – is the stored free-to-use stock of drawings available on your word processor. Microsoft's clipart tool can also connect you, if you go on-line (that is, connect to the internet), to a hugely increased choice of images to browse through. Once you *copy and paste* an image it's easy to *re-size* it. The computer calls clipart pictures "bit-maps", and gives their files the suffix **.bmp** (*the file extension*).

clipboard The "clipboard" is non-material – the term is borrowed from the physical or 'real' world – and is the part of electronic memory in the word processor program for temporary storage of text and images which have been either copied or cut. (See *cut, copy, paste*). The copied or cut text remains in this temporary location ('on the clipboard') until overwritten by the next *copy* or *cut* action, regardless of how many times you might *paste* that text to other places in (any) documents. If you are closing down the word processor with text still on the clipboard, the program will likely ask if you want to keep it there for next time, or discard it. Clipboard is an extremely useful element of the word processing program. In the newer versions of MSWord, clicking the Clipboard arrow symbol (in the menu, Home, furthest left) will bring up a pane showing what's currently stored on the clipboard.

code In *HTML* there are pieces of code which can readily be copied and dropped into another application, to get a programme to perform certain actions. An example would be if I wanted a webpage to have a tiny clock in one corner, and had seen it working elsewhere. I'd need to find the source of the code for that modification, acquire it, then insert it into the correct place in the HTML code of instructions which built my webpage or pages.

code monkey is computer slang for a person who earns money writing computer code. Compare *web monkey.*

computer   Something that computes, a data-processing machine. This is a note on the way we have used words for the thing we know as a computer. First there were calculators, starting centuries ago with the abacus—those sliding beads on hair or wires—and later mechanical adding machines. Electronic *calculators* got better and smaller. From the late 1940s there were computers which filled large rooms, and they came to be known as *mainframe computers,* or simply *mainframes.* The company IBM (International Business Machines)—faced with intense competition—brought out its computer small enough to fit on a desk; hence *desktop personal computer,* or desktop, or PC. Then other companies came out with "IBM clones"—personal computers compatible with the software most in use. An exception was the **Apple** company which developed a separate operating system, and gained and retained a loyal following. Apple were first to have a "graphical interface" in the 1980s, adopted by all since.

For years the two operating systems remained mutually exclusive and software was designed just for one or the other. These days it's possible to get versions of most programs to suit PC or Mac, or even to install compatibility software.

Things scaled down even more in size (but not in computing power) to arrive at the *laptop computer* (or just laptop), from various manufacturers, and next came a generation of palmtop computers and a whole bunch of proprietary named devices; iPods, iPads, iPhones etc. What's more, most cars or cellphones today are each likely to have greater installed computer capacity than, for instance, the successful Apollo Eleven moon mission of 1969.

Control Key, Ctrl The Control key, usually marked **Ctrl** on a modern keyboard, sits at either end of the bottom row of main keys. Some keyboards may mark it with a "caret", that is, an upward pointing arrowhead sign. It is known as a modifier key, and seldom has an effect on its own. You use it in conjunction with certain other keys. Examples: Ctrl+s = save (your work); Ctrl+p = print; Ctrl+i = italicize (after you've highlighted the text you select); Ctrl+b = **bold**. The last two actions are repeated to undo. That is, to remove the italic or bolding, respectively. In older systems, Ctrl+ Alt + Delete was an emergency keystroke combination to close a "frozen" computer when all else failed – other than pulling the plug. Doing that today gets you the equivalent of a pained look of disdain from the computer, as if to say,"Oh c'mon! Get real."

Control Panel Press **Start** on your computer's start-up (welcome) page: this brings up a menu which should have **Control Panel** as one of the options. Click on that, then you see a box which will show many icons for things such as Date & Time, Display, Keyboard, Mouse, and probably many more. These are worth exploring. You can re-set various options in **Display**. You can check that **Date & Time** are correct for your time zone. **Keyboard** and **Mouse** will simply say that the computer recognizes the make and function of those hardware items: you don't need to take any action on those. In short, Control Panel has much to show you, and to offer.

copy In word processing, the typist or keyboarder will often want to copy quickly and easily, rather than re-type, long passages of text. The copying can be done from any place within the same document, or from a quite different source. The simple procedure just needs a *highlighting* of the passage to be copied, a RIGHT cllick of the mouse, a LEFT click on the word **Copy** which appears in the list, then another left click at the place you want to insert the passage. This will **paste** the copied material. That's a **copy and paste** action. The original text stays where it was. You created a new copy. Sounds hard, but the action becomes second nature after only a few tries. Another sense of the word "copy" – text written for a client, often for advertising purposes – is frequently encountered in the computer and internet context.

corrupt   It isn't a moral judgment. Any messed up text, file, instruction or code is said in computer-lingo to be corrupt.

crash Oops, the computer fell off the piano. No, seriously, the computer crashes when it stops doing what you want it to do, and shuts itself down when you had other plans. Worse is when it freezes or locks up and fails to respond, even if asked nicely to "close". Darn. You may then have to crash it deliberately, by switching off mains power, relying upon the computer's ability to re-start with its systems intact. Twenty years ago this meant big trouble. Computers have gotten smarter. A frozen *laptop* computer might not close down: it was connected to mains (house-power) electricity which you then switched off. But the pesky thing has its own battery, and won't shut down. The only solution in that case may be to take out the battery, have a quiet lie down to recover composure, then a strong coffee, and start over. What? You wanted a hi-tech answer?

CreateSpace.com CS is a business wholly owned by Amazon.com and if you experiment with self-publishing by going here, you can design a book and will be asked, when your material is ready, to *upload* a *PDF* file. Not too hard. Type your text in a normal Word document and, when done, hit 'Save As' – one of the options that comes up is, "Save as a PDF file." Follow the on-site instructions. This book is an example of a CreateSpace product.

cut Perhaps even more commonly required than *copy and paste* (see above) and just as easy, you perform a **cut** in the same way as **copy** except you click on the word cut, not copy, when opening the edit list with a right click. You **paste** in the same way. You have performed **cut and paste**. However, unlike *copy and paste*, you have removed (cut) the piece of text from its original location, and unless you place it elsewhere, with a **paste**, it will be gone forever when you close the word processor. Meanwhile, it sits in the *clipboard*.

CPU That's the Central Processing Unit, which is the brainy chip (microprocessor) the size of a thumb nail at the heart of a computer.

D

data compression See *zipfile*

defragment, "de-frag" Running a defrag program lets the computer tidy up its hard disc, so that scattered pieces of electronically related data are grouped closer together, and this is meant to remedy a tendency to slow down, which comes about as *clusters* of information on the hard drive became fragmented. In part, that happens because each time we "delete" something we don't actually delete anything – merely mark it as OK to over-write. One result is that, over time, the hard drive gets cluttered by odd bits of data in umpteen places.

Delicious (formerly del.icio.us, pronounced "delicious") is a social *bookmarking* web service for storing, sharing, and discovering web bookmarks. The site was founded by Joshua Schachter in 2003 and acquired by Yahoo! in 2005. By the end of 2008, the service claimed more than 5.3 million users and 180 million unique *bookmarked* URLs. (from *Wikipedia*)

desktop Two meanings. First, it is short for desktop computer, that is, the PC itself. But the computer's *desktop* also refers to the opening display on your screen, plus the program which allows an accumulation of various little icons which are *shortcuts* to different programs or files that you might use often.

Note that if the visual clutter becomes too much, it's harmless to remove the shortcut icons. It doesn't affect the program which the shortcut had pointed to. To remove a shortcut icon from the desktop, right-click on it, then click "delete". As I said, that only deletes the icon, NOT the program.

desktop publishing (DTP) is a general term (no longer used so much as before) referring to the layout and production of text and imagery, using word-processing and in some cases a sophisticated design software. The intended output can be posters, signage, or other display material, as well as actual published brochures, reports or books, using the resources of a PC with *peripherals* like a printer and binder. The printing part of such an operation could be outsourced. Or, the desktop publisher might deliver work electronically to the other side of the world as an element in a larger publishing enterprise. It is characteristic that this publishing is of smaller scale than old-style businesses using large printeries. **DTP** is something of a catch-all label.

dialog box   When some programs are opened, they display a square-shaped box or panel with various queries asking you to respond with information, to allow the program to proceed. Commercial sites might try to get more info from you than is needed to run the program. In effect they are *phishing. (e.g. "Thanks for signing for this newsletter. Check the boxes below to let us know which other magazines or products you are interested in.")* Be prepared to ignore it. Leave unchecked/unticked anything that seems intrusive and not the reason you came to the site. Most dialog boxes are sensible and relevant.

disc burner, see *burner*

display   The display is just what you see, and how you see it, on the screen. For example, you might go to *control panel* , click on *display*, then on *screensaver*, and choose to have the monitor show a pleasant landscape scene if the computer is left unattended for 5 minutes; then to change the scene every 30 seconds. You decide the settings.

dithering   An image is dithered by a graphics program when – to the human eye – it is smoothed out at the edges. Thus we can get an even-looking curve on a graph, or a gradation of colors at color boundaries to make a realistic image, drawn or photographic.

document   No mystery here. In a word-processing program, you open a file which has as its title a name of your choosing. You look at, or work on, whatever document is in the file, and afterwards close it. Plus, you probably did the smart thing and have the file located in a named folder of related files.

DOS   The letters stand for Disc Operating System, especially in relation to the typical operating systems of the computers of the 1980s, which required typed commands of a not-very-user-friendly kind.

download   Another computer sends something to your computer. Download is what you do every time you get stuff from a computer connected to yours via a *network*. For something small like an email, this probably happens without anyone bothering to call it a download. But when a company, whose software your computer uses, brings out an updated version, you'll most likely be prompted by a screen message asking "Do you want to download the latest version of . . . ?" Any time you buy new software online, there will be a process for downloading after paying. See also *upload*

Dreamweaver was well-known, but fairly expensive, in the late 1990s as a website design software. One other such software was *Pagemaker*. Now the most popular website builder is *WordPress*.

DVDs, and **DVD player software** A DVD is a Digitised Versatile Disc. DVDs arrived as the step up from the basic CD (compact disc) for music or speech, just as they had taken over from cassettes of magnetic tape which are still around, whereas the once common reel-to-reel tapes won't be found now in ordinary stores.

We enjoy watching movies at home, using a DVD player, a monitor screen, and the inserted DVD . The screen can be on a small or large TV, or on a dedicated player. Your computer too is quite capable of playing your DVDs. The computer just needs the software to do it, and there are several programs available. More than one can be available on the same computer. For example, Windows Media Player is something like a standard, produced as the name suggests by the Windows family of Microsoft's products. You might have, as your machine's operating system, XP, Vista, Windows 7 or a successor. All will have Windows Media Player installed.

Examples of companies that produce media-playing software, downloadable to home computers, are Ashampoo and Nero.

Another media-player software is *Quicktime*, from the Apple company, which also has versions able to run on PCs, that is, not just on Apple computers.

E

eBay Inc is the multi-billion dollar company that made online auctions big business. Many individuals and companies routinely buy and sell via eBay. Founder in 1995 was Pierre Omidyar. Operations are localized in 30 countries.

e-commerce is the convenient term for any electronically conducted business. Some businesses are almost exclusively e-businesses, while few now operate with no computer-assisted activity. Anyone who ever uses a bank's automatic teller machine (ATM) is playing a part in e-commerce.

email The word email is simply *electronic mail* abbreviated to e-mail, now usually just written as email. What started as letters—either personal or for business—sent over the telephone lines (which is what happens) has become more sophisticated, so that we can send and receive *attachments* with our emails, like *digital photographs* or long documents in *PDF format,* as well as *forwarded email.* For many internet users, email is the major benefit and day-to-day reason for having an internet connection.

Enter key Some keyboards may still say "Return" based on the old "carriage return" wording on typewriters which reveal the ancestry of computer keyboards. Hitting "Enter" is the moment when our prepared computer action is put into effect, and can't always be undone, so we should try to be sure of what we plan will happen. It could be anything from simply skipping a line and starting a new paragraph, to deleting a large amount of highlighted text (as a *block*) or setting in motion a big download, making an online purchase and entering into a contract.

encryption When people buy things online, the transactions (usually by credit card) are encrypted for security, and we have to trust that it all works. The computer user at home doesn't need to do anything technical. Many users remain reluctant to trust money transaction via the internet. One alternative to credit cards is using a company such as *PayPal* for buying and/or selling. They act as intermediaries, and *they* have your account and card details, but the merchants from whom you buy do not.

Esc key (or **Esc**)   This key usually is at the top left of the keyboard. The lettering stands for Escape. It's not because you become frustrated enough to want to run off. The Escape key may do several things, sometimes in conjunction with other keys. It is a left-over from earlier days when it could activate commands in computing routines, otherwise given as No, Quit, Exit, Stop, Cancel, Abort – commands which nowadays are done more or less automatically in various applications. Online, **Esc** often works to pause or go back from some procedure: a common example is if you watch a downloaded video in full-screen mode. **Esc** will return the view to a small window (where you can see the other options which had been unavailable while watching in full-screen) Fortunately, if you press Esc and nothing happens, there's no harm done. Try something else!.

Excel   This is the name of Microsoft's popular *spreadsheet* software . It comes with the Microsoft Office suite.

Excite was one of the most recognized 'Internet portals' of the 1990s and its search-engine rivalled *Yahoo!* and *Lycos*. Today the company is more diversified. It is said to be developing a search engine dedicated to rock'n'roll music. Famous too for refusing to buy *Google* for $1m in 1998.

F

Facebook   This is the name of the biggest *social network service* website, founded by Mark Zuckerberg and fellow Harvard students and launched in 2004; now open to anyone 13 or over. Users create personal profiles and exchange details and news. Facebook has become the second biggest website in the world, claimed to have 500 million active users as at mid-2010; beaten out for top spot only by *Google*. It is blocked in some countries (China, Iran, North Korea, Syria and Vietnam) and at workplaces where bosses detect unacceptable timewasting by employes spending their time on Facebook.

fax   (short for facsimile) You might have a separate fax machine at home or office. However, the computer, with an appropiate scanner and software, can do the same job.

file   (file as in filing cabinet) A file can be a *document* or a *spreadsheet* and needs to be uniquely named so the computer can recognize and retrieve it. See *folder*.

file extension   File extensions are the fiddly 3-letter endings to otherwise sensible-looking file names, and are always preceded by a dot. Say, I've called my latest file Letters to Grandma. The computer calls it, without even asking, Letters to Grandma.**docx** What the -- ?! So then I see that all my ordinary documents get the same treatment. The ending, the file extension, is .doc or .docx for lots of stuff. A few are **.pdf** and I soon work out that they are the e-books I can read with the Adobe Acrobat software. My photos have some fancy ID number with an ending **.jpg** and other drawn images turn out to be **.bmp**. Maybe I get an email download saying it's a **.txt** (yes, that was short for 'text'). Ah, so they DO mean something! The main thing is that the computer needs to keep the files tracked in its own way, in addition to YOUR naming of some files. Believe me, this is a good thing. It's handy to recognize the sort of material that's in a file by noticing the file extension, but it's no big deal.

Find and Replace is a useful tool in the word-processor MSWord. By nominating a given exact word or phrase – that is, any set of characters – you can ask the computer program to substitute another word or phrase, of your choosing, everywhere it occurs in the document. Imagine the convenience: you discover that you've spelt an important recurring name wrongly, throughout a whole 150-page report. With **Find and Replace**, a couple of clicks and it's fixed.

flatbed scanner   see *scanner*

flaming You don't often hear this term used any longer. Talking to each other in *chat rooms* – by typing text – some individuals wrote plenty of strong language and swearing, and still do. But flaming was when one or more members were particularly offensive to another member, often a new member, with the obvious aim of driving them away.

Webmasters and the moderators of the chat rooms now will not tolerate such behavior. You'll see it written into the conditions for being in the group, that no malicious abuse directed at others (i.e. flaming) is acceptable. There can still be robust discussion!

floppy discs The older 5¼ inch floppies have become museum pieces. The 3½ inch floppy disc is still around. Funny name, because the hard plastic shell or case is hard. The floppy bit of plastic with the encoded information is safe inside. For portable data (digitized photos, charts, documents

… anything) a *memory stick* replaces what once would have needed hundreds of 1.44Mb floppy discs.

folder   Meaningfully named folders in your word processor are where you should place your files, which in turn contain the documents of words and images, or a *spreadsheet*, being worked on, or which you are keeping for reference.

The words **file** and **folder**, just like the little icons on the screen, mirror the physical files, folders or documents familiar from the traditional business office. Early on it may not seem important, but as you create more and more documents (even just your archive of snailmail letters that you printed and sent) you soon will appreciate having everything neatly **kept** and easily **retrieved**.

G

games and **gamers** There are essentially two kinds of games to play on the screen of the computer. First there's the stand-alone type of game which probably came pre-loaded on your hard-drive (Solitaire is the best-known: I have known it to give great satisfaction to older first-time computer users; it is even regarded sometimes as an ideal "way in" to computers.) and dozens more of that category which can be downloaded from many Internet sites. Some of these can be played with more than one player, in the manner of chess or checkers or versions of classic arcade games.

Then there are the online role-play games where the players – gamers – engage in contest as characters in the virtual world. The real-life players, many in the same game, could be in just about any country. Through their online characters, or *avatars*, they might be battling in *World of Warcraft*, or in a game scenario where they are trying to built a political empire, or further a career in any undertaking. It is an absorbing activity for thousands of computer users. See also *Steam*.

gaming Different from either of the above is actual gambling-type gaming, where the participants are playing online – for real money – in a well simulated casino environment. Electronic betting established its credentials early in the piece with horse-racing. A camera's eye view of a horse race in real time makes this something of a natural for on-screen betting/gaming.

Gates Bill Gates founded his company Microsoft when desktop computers were – fairly briefly – known as "micro computers" to distinguish them from room-sized mainframes.

He was a software developer of operating systems. Micro+Soft ... get it? The corporate history of the company, its battles with Federal legislation, its capture of 90% of world market for its successive operating systems for IBM-clone PCs, is a saga for several large volumes and not two paragraphs. **Bill Gates** of Microsoft and **Steve Jobs** of Apple are the only individuals with their own entries in this book. It would have been a bit ridiculous to leave them out. However, this is not a bio book!   P.S. Both these men were geeks. (see next word ⇨)

geek   A formerly slang word now gone mainstream, meaning a technically savvy person, like the older "boffin'.

generation Like other things in the realms both of biology and engineering, computer hardware is said to evolve in generations. In the 1990s when microchips had names like 486, we were in the fourth generation and since then have moved on thru a fifth generation.

Gmail   Gmail is a free-to-use email service provided by Google since 2007.

Google   Company co-founders Sergey Brin and Larry Page originally called their start-up company BackRub (the search engine emphasised "back-links") and arrived at the name Google via a spelling misunderstanding, which is as good a way as any. Before Google was incorporated (Sept. 1998) the company *Excite* had walked away from a chance to buy the search engine for $750,000. Page and Brin offered to sell because they wanted to get on with their academic studies, But by the end of 2004 Google had reached market capitalization of $23billion. It is the biggest web-based company on Earth. Major dictionaries now include the verb "to google".

grayscale   Your computer's printer can be set to print in color, or black only, or grayscale which is when shades of gray are used in order to convey something of the varied look and texture of a color document, but using only the black ink.

gutters   The gutters are the blank space at the inside edge of printed pages, nearest the spine when it becomes a bound document – specifically, a book. Your computer's word processor (like MS Word) is capable of multiple settings for page and print options, including specifying gutter details.

H

hackers and **hacking** Hacker (originally an admiring term) is the name given to a skilled person who may see as a challenge the security measures put into place by serious players like banks and the Defense Department. Getting past other people's passwords (hacking their computer) is just one particular game. Occasionally, high profile cases receive media attention.

hardware Your computer sitting on the table or in its metal *tower* on the floor, or an electronic organizer in a briefcase, are all examples of hardware. Same goes for the computer's *mouse,* the *keyboard,* a *webcam,* the *screen,* an *external harddrive.* They're all physical, touchable . . . they are the hardware. See also *software,* meaning the electronic programs which you can't actually see happening—just the results as they appear on your screen.

headset & **headphones** Most of us have a clear idea of what the wearing of a pair of **headphones** looks like, even the slim kind you'd have used with your old Walkman cassette player. But a **headset** also has a microphone – on a swivel-stalk – in addition to the padded earphones. And you can talk to others online via *Skype,*

highlight Moving the mouse across text while the left mouse-button is held down, creates **highlighting**, anything from a single character to as many pages as you wish. The next action (e.g. making **bold**, or making *italic*, copying or deleting) will then apply to the entire highlighted area (block).

hits In internet parlance a hit means a visit to a website, by anyone who comes to that address either directly by typing or pasting the address, or by a link from elsewhere. A site is largely rated by how many visits (i.e. hits) it receives.

housekeeping is general maintenance and the tidy keeping of *files* as well as seeing to other things such as protection against computer *viruses*, *defragging* from time to time, etc.

HTML HyperText Markup Language. The fancy name doesn't matter. We ordinary users don't write in HTML code, but there are professional coders, and they assure us that it is not as arcane as we think. A blogging *platform* like Blogspot.com lets its members use HTML when posting blog material, **or** to write in plain language, referred to as *WYSIWYG*, "what you see is what you get."

http HyperText Transfer Protocol. A mystic bunch of letters is at the front of most internet addresses, mostly in the form **http://** (the letters followed by a colon and two forward slashes.) The variant **https** has the added **s** which indicates extra security. You could meet **ftp** for File Transfer Protocol.

hyperlink A hyperlink is an *active link* to a website. Instead of the intending visitor needing to type in, or *cut and paste*, the address provided, he or she simply clicks on the link, for example from someone's blog or an email. If it's an active link (hyperlink) the person clicking it is taken straight to the new site, provided that the link was set up correctly by the person creating it.

I

ink cartrldge and **inkjet**   See **printer**

Internet   "Internet," "The 'Net" or "The Web" are terms now used interchangeably. It is usually optional to capitalize the words. It refers to a global electronic network to which our computers at home can connect, through a small device called a *modem,* and with the help of an *ISP* company (internet service provider) for a fee. The internet can let you send and receive *emails* and do much else, including transacting business.

What we now call the Internet started in the 1970s experimentally as a link-up of the computers of several universities—and military intelligence—and now is like a living thing worldwide and open to all, despite attempts by authoritarian jurisdictions to control people's use of it for general communication and the sharing of ideas and information.

iPhone4   A state of the art hand-held computer & phone device from the Apple company, introduced by CEO Steve Jobs (see following article) at the 2010 Worldwide Developers Conference.

J

Jobs, Steven Paul Steve Jobs, (born 1955) is the co-founder and boss of Apple Inc. He is a phenomenon of the corporate computing world, blending technical knowhow, creative and esthetic imagination, and business acumen. Some would add ruthlessness. His personal story is remarkable – born of Near Eastern parentage and with adoptive American parents. As a high-schooler he became fascinated by computer technology and attended out-of-hours classes run by the Hewlett Packard company. At just 16 he formed an association with Steve Wozniak, 5 years his senior, and they together with a third co-founder, Mike Markkula, went on to start up the company that became Apple. They created the Apple II computer and then the Apple Macintosh. The rest, as they say, is history.

Even more extraordinary, Jobs was ousted in a board-room maneuver (1985) but then started another tech-whiz company (NeXT) and in1986 acquired the computer graphics division of Lucasfilm which was turned into Pixar Animation Studios.

New techniques of animation were behind Pixar's successful movies for the Walt Disney Company – five Academy Awards for Best Animation from these; Toy Story, A Bug's Life, Toy Story 2, Monsters Inc, Finding Nemo, The Incredibles, Ratatouille, WALL-E, Cars, Up, Toy Story 3. The advances were largely due to Jobs's range of skills, both technical and entrepreneurial. When Apple acquired Pixar, Steve Jobs got the top job and has since remained CEO. On top of that, he achieved a 15% share of Disney, the biggest individual shareholding in that iconic company following its acquisition of Pixar in 2006.

Jobs's personal wealth is in the billions – something ever-fascinating to celebrity watchers. And he certainly defines the category of a Silicon Valley celeb.

The Wikipedia article on Steve Jobs includes the following:

"Jobs' history in business has contributed much to the symbolic image of the idiosyncratic, individualistic Silicon Valley entrepreneur, emphasizing the importance of design and understanding the crucial role aesthetics play in public appeal. His work driving forward the development of products that are both functional and elegant has earned him a devoted following.

Jobs is listed as either primary inventor or co-inventor in over 230 awarded patents or patent applications related to a range from actual computer and portable devices to user interfaces (including touch-based), speakers, keyboards, power adapters, staircases, clasps, sleeves, lanyards and packages."

Those last couple of lines contain a bunch of terms which refer to internal computer *architecture*. Guess what. No need to waste your time looking them up in this book!

K

keyboard A quick glance tells us that the computer keyboard is visually not unlike the traditional typewriter keyboard. Former typists who might have used an electric IBM "golf ball" typewriter had little trouble transferring their keyboarding skills to a computer environment. New with computers was the top row of Function keys (F1 to F12) which allow valuable short cuts, or abbreviated sets of instructions (*macros*) when used with either of the Alt keys found on left and right side of the space bar, at the bottom of the keyboard. Some keyboards are wireless, communicating remotely with the user's computer.

L

label-making Some inkjet printers come with label-maker software for designing and printing various labels, not only typical shapes for address labels etc, but capable of printing rounded shapes to fit a CD or DVD. Some other printers have the means to print directly onto white-topped discs; others again can use a "light scribe" method for inscribing metallic discs.

languages Thank goodness we ordinary computer users do not have anything to do with those programming languages we used to hear about when computers were mentioned – names like Fortran, Cobol, Algol, or even BASIC (which stands for Beginner's All-purpose Symbolic Instruction Code)! English works just fine, with or without your *spellcheckers*. An amazing thing is that nearly all the main natural languages and their distinctive writing systems are available, for word-processing applications and for internet use: Arabic, Chinese (both traditional and simplified forms), Greek, Hebrew, Japanese, Korean, European languages with versions of the Latin alphabet; Slavic scripts for Russian and its relatives; then there's Hindi, Tamil, Thai ... many more. When you go to various websites, they may offer versions in dozens of languages. See also *translation*.

laptop The so-called laptop portable computers of the late 1980s were as heavy as some of the old typewriters. New lightweight laptops may now be found in the schoolbags of primary-age children. They are likely to have wireless internet connections, and have few if any limitations in comparison with their larger desktop cousins.

login or **log-in** To log in to any computer program is simply to identify yourself with a previously agreed user ID and, if asked for, a password. Every program has its own criteria. For some, your identity (ID) may be expressed as a special word or nickname, or your regular name, or (very commonly) the email address by which you joined that program. Many users manage to acquire several email addresses, so it's a good idea to keep track of which email addresses are used to join up in what programs. In other words, treat all such information as you would a note of the relevant passwords. They add up!

long-tail A long-tail keyword or phrase is what you're typing into a search engine such as Google if you are searching using three or more words, especially if you enclose them in inverted commas which makes yours an "exact search." YOU don't need to know it's called a long-tail (or long tailed) keyword search, but it is of great interest to marketers to know that you do such searches. Example: you type *cruise holidays.* Your search will produce a heap of websites of agencies keen to book you on a cruise holiday to …somewhere. But if you search *"Alaska cruises 2012",* not only does this make YOU sound like a serious buyer who knows what he or she wants, it will produce more exact search results. However, if a person wants to conduct more open searches, they should omit the inverted commas.

Lycos Lycos Inc, founded 1994, was an early player with – as well as other e-business – an excellent search engine. In 1999 it was the most-visited internet destination on the planet. In 2000 it was bought for upwards of five billion dollars by Spanish telco Terra Networks, merging to become Terra Lycos, just as the "internet bubble" was about to burst.

In 2004 Korea's Daum Communications acquired part of this company for a dramatically reduced sum of $96 million, and re-established Lycos Inc. On August 16, 2010, Ybrant Digital of India (but controlled by Warren Buffett's group Berkshire Hathaway) announced the signing of a stock purchase agreement to acquire Lycos Inc. for $36 million.

M

macro An enigmatic term but it only means a set of (computer) instructions which are set in train by a single command, to run a program. In practise, the user gets to do a one-click action and the computer does the rest, then tells you "I'm done." An example is the File-cleaner program (a macro) if it is attached to MSWord as an *add-in*.

malware Partly it's a play on the word software, but more to the point, malware is **harmful** software, possibly introduced to the computer belonging to a buyer of an innocent-seeming program. This is probably not a virus as such; the malware might be designed to "spy" on your activities for commercial advantage.

mark as Each time you check out your email there are several actions you can pick from the menu along the top line, and this is pretty similar for the various browsers (Firefox Gmail, Hotmail, Internet Explorer, Netscape, etc). To open an email you simply click on the email's subject line, the line that hopefully tells you what the email's about.

However, if you are about to perform a special action, first check (tick) the box to the left of an email subject-line. Then you can hit "delete" without even opening that email; or "junk", which instructs that all messages from THAT sender will go to a junk folder (where you can still retrieve them if you change your mind); and the **mark as** label is often useful. Click on it to bring down another menu of choices – (mark as) unread; (mark as) *spam*; (mark as) important / to be followed up. The different browsers use different wording and ways to highlight the subject line, so as to catch your eye next time you look at the emails in your "mailbox".

You get used to your own browser and email system very quickly, and can always change to another if you want. Many computer users have two or more email providers.

media Newspapers, books, magazines ... they are print media. Media is a plural word. Each is a medium of communication. "The media" is a term to include all the channels of communication. Electronic media are radio, TV, telephones and . . . the internet.

microprocessor otherwise known as a "computer chip" is the effective brain of a computer, able to process data at lightning speed. I have no idea how. Go ask a geek.

modem Your computer probably has an internally installed modem even if it has not been activated so as to communicate with an internet service provider (ISP). But many users own an external modem. The word was created from the technical term "modulator/de-modulator" which has no relevance here unless you want to chase it up for more techie information, or show off to your kids. Which never works anyway. All that matters is that you will need a modem for when you feel ready to get on the internet. Once up and running, your modem will either be invisible inside the computer tower, or else it'll sit there happily blinking its little green lights at you. A case of "set and forget."

motherboard Possibly you will never see one. It (or she?) is there, as the heart and soul of your computer, the physical frame or apparatus that holds the intelligent microprocessor chip and its principal connections within the tower or computer case [e.g. the connections to the *ports* (outlets at the back), or to the tray for CDs and DVDs etc.]

mouse   The computer mouse is a friendly little guy. It and the keyboard act as the "interface" between you and the computer — the way you and the computer talk to each other. There are wireless mice, as well as the older kind with wires which I guess are a bit like tails. It's OK to call these kinds of mice "mouses". Nobody much minds.

Be aware that your mouse can do a (single) "click", or a "double click", and also allows "left click" and "right click", which do different things. You can even set double-click to suit your personal clicking speed. Sounds confusing. Quite important to pay attention to, but all this soon comes naturally.

iPhone4 and similar smartphone hand-held computer devices have sought to dispense entirely with the mouse, giving the user touch-screen manipulation via a fingertip-flick action.

Laptop computers too, may use tracker-balls or touch pads, but some are happy to have a mouse plugged into them. If you lose your mouse, you could try luring it back with a piece of cheese left on the computer desk overnight. I haven't heard of this actually working, but there's always a first time.

N

Netscape Search is the *search engine* of the Netscape company, which has a popular *browser*.

network   In an office environment most of the computer screens (probably referred to as work station terminals, or other fancy term) might be linked by an internal system of cabled connections. That's a network, or LAN for *local area network*. However, for home users, the biggest network by far is the *internet,* which is global, and not the property of any one owner.

niche Whether you know it or not, most every time someone advertises to you, they regard you as belonging in a *niche* or special group (such as "over 50," or "teen," or "golfer") to help them sell you a product. Either that or they are trying to find out what niche you ARE in. This is especially so with internet advertising.

O

OCR That's "optical character recognition". Your computer may have OCR software which you can use in conjunction with a flatbed scanner. Unlike with photocopying a document, the scanner will scan and the OCR program will try to read the text of the document and save it as text . You can then convert it to any font you may want, or for that matter cut, copy, paste, edit any of the text. A problem is that any blobs or blots on the original paper sheet, and any unclear letters, will cause the OCR program to make a guess at what it most looks like, and you can get some weird results. In other words, be willing to edit the result carefully.

operating systems Whereas there are operating systems favored by computer-savvy technicians and designers, such as *Linux* (pron. LINN-uhks), and more, the hugely successful Microsoft company captured over 90% of the world market with successive launches of its operating systems, going back to the predecessors of Windows 95, Win 97, Windows 2000, thru XP, Vista, Windows 7. Microsoft was always a *software* company, not a computer manufacturer.

Apple Inc, by contrast, builds its own brand of computers and installs its own operating system (OS X).

Apple has about 5% of the world market, which is big by normal standards of "market penetration", except that this pales when compared to the Microsoft giant.

Computer people talk about such and such an operating system being the "platform" on which software programs run.

open source software (OSS) There are complexities around the technical and legal aspects of **open source**

software; and besides, the term 'open source' seems to mean a few different things. It's worth noting that the concept has a considerable movement behind it. The wish is for an ethical free sharing of software-writing code and other things which private interests often try to gain control over, even if they did not do the main work to develop the software programs involved. *Wikipedia* says: *"Open source software is very often developed in a public, collaborative manner. Open-source software is the most prominent example of open source development and often compared to (technically defined) user-generated content or (legally defined) open content movements."*

opt-in   You may be asked to **opt-in** to a membership or a subscription, meaning "sign-up for", or even be guided to do so twice (in return for receiving some offered benefit such as a free download of an e-book), in which case it's called a "double opt-in". The online vendor or marketer has reasons for trying to get the details of enquirers or first-time customers. The details (a name and email) are worth money, even if they don't buy. An opt-in list of prospects is more valued than a "cold" list; a double opt-in list more valued yet.

outsourcing   You have already heard of the practise of outsourcing in business or government. It's all the go these days. Well, the internet is just the same. It is quite likely that that online promo you last read was advertising copy written by someone in India or the Philippines, and not the vendor of the product somewhere in the U.S. Of course, the maker of a product could also be . . . just about anywhere!

Overture   Another proprietary search-engine company.

P

pagebreak means 'begin a new page'. In all word-processing, documents are automatically 'broken' into pages, that is, split or divided to fit the printed page according to the size of the selected *font,* and other factors. But a **pagebreak** can be set manually at <u>any</u> desired place in the document. (In MSWord, click on Insert, then on Pagebreak.)

PageMaker is a website design software by Aldus, a company which is now owned by *Adobe*.

password Any time you're asked to set (create) a password please don't enter the word "password" itself. You'd probably find that it is not accepted. [See too the entry under QWERTY.] You will be asked in most cases to **set** your desired password with a minimum of six letters or numerals, or mix of the two. Then a screen message will say if it's considered weak, good, or strong (or equivalent wording). You'll be informed of any symbols that are not allowed—it is certain that a forward slash (/) or a colon (:) are not acceptable. *Case sensitive?* Not case sensitive? Setting your passwords can be a lot of fun.

Then there is more fun each time you need to **give** (that is, type in) your password for access to whatever it may be you **want** access to! Did you make an accurate note of what you originally **set** as the password? I sure hope so. Make it a habit. And remember *Caps Lock*? Don't leave it on by mistake, or you'll wonder why a known password is rejected.

paste When you *cut* or *copy* anything from a document in the word processor, you often wish to place the material elsewhere in the same, or another, document. You do so by clicking with the mouse at the intended new location, then right-click to show the drop-down menu, and left-click on the word **paste**. You check to see if it all went well, and make any corrections needed.

PayPal   This company, owned by eBay since 2002, is a major provider of money transfer services. Instead of online buyers giving their credit card or bank account details to each seller, PayPal acts as intermediary, and customers feel a benefit from easier password-protected transactions. Card details are not shared with the sellers. The service works also for payments <u>received</u> by the account-holder. (It was three former employes of PayPal who set up the extraordinarily fast-growing *YouTube* in 2005.)

PDF file Portable Document Format. In effect, a "locked" text in a cannot-be-edited form. These files have the suffix **.pdf**

peripherals The word just means generally "(the things) around (something else)" hence in relation to a computer, its peripheral hardware – the peripherals – will include printer, mouse, keyboard, monitor, speakers, a headset, any external harddrive, external modem, webcam, and other temporary connections such as a digital still or movie camera uploading to the computer. Peripheral describes the relationship, not the object. Don't say to a computer-store assistant, "I'd like a peripheral, please." (Of course, an alert and smart salesperson would reply, "Certainly. What color?")

phishing   This word is pronounced "fishing." Someone is trying to get you to provide personal information beyond what they have any right to know. The most blatant phishing is attempted through emails pretending to come from a high-profile source (big-name banks, for example), and claiming that "for security reasons" they need you to confirm certain details. Run a mile! This is fraudulent and, in bad cases where people are fooled, it leads to identity theft and other abuse. Consider reporting to the real institution that you have received these messages. They probably know already but will appreciate hearing from you. As an individual there is little you can do, other than NOT be taken for a ride. Never respond to dubious emails and NEVER OPEN AN ATTACHMENT that comes with such an email. You're not in too much danger simply reading an email which turns out to be, or you suspect to be, bogus/phoney. The same advise applies to all security issues. Computer *viruses* and other nasties are a total pain.

Picasa Software developed by Idealab and owned by Google since 2004, described as an image viewer for organizing and editing digital photographs. Google offers it as a free download. Recently started computer users are bound to keep hearing new names. Don't stress about it. Names will become familiar as you find what suits your activities.

pixel Computer screens (really, monitor screens) display their images made up of thousands of little dots called pixels. The word pixel is derived from "picture element". Since the computer can control the color and intensity of each pixel, the entire screen image is created with precision.

platform Any program needs an underlying base or platform which allows it to perform. This 'platform' – as usual a word has been pressed into service from the physical world – consists of an electronic system which is likely to be the *operating system* for the computer involved. Thus, an Apple Mac piece of software will not run on a *Windows* platform.

plugin   A plug-in consists of a software program that adds some kind of extra ability to an existing program. Plug-ins are commonly used in a web browser to scan for viruses, or maybe play video. This is nice to know, but it has little to do with the ordinary computer user, who just enjoys what **it** does and does not have to **do** anything more to make it happen.

port   Your computer has outlets (normally in back of the tower etc) called ports, that are there for plugging in the cables from various devices. The *USB* connectors have become the standard, which makes matters a lot easier.

Portal is the name of an award-winning computer game (it can be played by a solo player) for Xbox 360 &Play Station 3. The idea of the game is to solve a series of puzzles encountered when a player's character goes through a "portal" in the science-fictional sense, by teleporting, and then – to complicate matters – is challenged by an Artificial Intelligence named GLaDOS. There is a Windows version of the game, and a Mac OS X version was released in mid-2010. Portal 2 will be released in early 2011 by *Valve Corporation*.

printer   Most home computer users have one or more *ink jet printers,* the current industry standard. Older technology might have had impact printers (daisy wheel type*)*. A typewriter, manual or electric, was an example of impact printing. Laser printers are available and more likely to be found in professional situations, such as in a design studio. In a printer itself, the **printer head** may last the life of the machine, but the user can expect to replace ink cartridges routinely, or – not always possible – refill ink reservoirs.

printer ink   The colors for printing are red, blue and yellow, plus black. This palette allows a full range of good color rendering. The home computer and printer today are together capable of printing high quality glossy photographic images, as well as high speed document printing in black & white, or full color, or *grayscale*.

Q

Quicken is a proprietary 'accounting package' software for tracking a business's inventory, costs and sales.

Quicktime is the media-player software created by the Apple company.

QWERTY This makes a pronounceable word – just say kwerty. Your typing keyboard or keypad is called a *qwerty* keyboard because of the first alphabetic letters appearing at upper left, carried over from the traditional typewriter. Did you ever wonder why the letters don't merely run a,b,c,d,e,f. . . . x,y,z? This was to do with finger positioning and frequency of hitting common combinations of letters. [A side note: so many internet users wanted to enter **qwerty** as a *password,* when a password was asked for, that it is now common for that combination of letters to be disallowed. Of course, this is up to each business owner or organization which wants you to enter a password to access its service. The other frequent "not allowed" is the word *password* itself. YOU can be more imaginative!]

R

RAM   RAM stands for random access memory, and while you and I don't need to know about the behind-the-scenes technical goings-on, having enough RAM is a big deal. Think of it as available active memory. It's what lets your computer think, as opposed to merely store scads of information (in its hard-drive memory). Back in the '80s and '90s, home computers kept running out of RAM-type memory when trying to do demanding jobs like graphics, which ate it up. This has become less of an issue, now that the available hardware is up to the task.

RealPlayer is a proprietary media player you can download to your computer, which plays a number of multimedia formats; MP3; MPEG-4; plus the same company's RealAudio and RealVideo; it also (being "cross-platform") can handle files made for playing on other media players.

re-size Re-sizing is what it says. You can normally change the size of screen images, and especially the text you are working on, in several ways. At the browser menu, click on View, then on Zoom (In or Out) for the preferred viewing size of what is on screen. To change the size of your own work in Microsoft Word, you can of course select – at the menu's Home – your font and font size, which offers a wide range. In addition, at the menu's View, you see a shortcut button to 100% size for the currently open document, and next to it a Zoom button which lets you pick any percentage with precision. But there is also a slider bar, at lower right of the screen, allowing a quick adjustment from 10% to 500%. For images, such as copy-pasted *clipart* pictures, once the pic is pasted into your document it's easy to click-on to highlight, then click-on one of the "handles" (they look like dots at the sides and corners of the highlighted picture) then drag the dot to change the size of the image. These are the sorts of thing that you can review in Help menu or in an on-screen Tutorial – plus some good-old practise, including trial and error, but to be polite we call it experimentation. What is it they say? There are no mistakes. There is only learning.

ROM The letters stand for read-only memory in reference to a type of electronic storage which the user cannot alter. Often encountered as CD-ROM, a compact disc which the user cannot "write to", as distinct from recordable and re-writable discs.

S

scanner   One very useful item of hardware is the scanner, and the most useful sort are flatbed scanners on which you can place anything (usually a book) face down as if on a photocopier. It'll do a straightforward copy job if that's all you want. The difference is that an image can also be transferred to the computer's memory. You thus have a digital file of the image, and later could make more copies without needing the original. Or you may wish to send the image to someone as an email attachment or as a fax. A scanner does all of that.   See also **OCR**

screen capture   See *screenshot*, below

screensaver   Click Start, then *control panel* then *display*, then **screensaver**. Picking any option other than 'none' will tell the computer to activate an animated display after a certain time, as chosen by you. This was intended to save your screen from "burn out" which was an issue with the classic cathode-ray-tube screens. Now users mainly like to see attractive images cycling as a "slide show" while a computer is not being worked at. The images can be your own pix retrieved by the screensaver program from your picture folders.

screenshot   A screenshot is simply an image of what's on a particular monitor screen. But you don't need a camera to "shoot" a picture of the TV or computer screen (although that is perfectly possible). Instead, with certain software, a couple of mouse clicks will allow "screen capture" of what's on the screen, that you wish to capture and display in a different way, perhaps incorporated in a video. See *Camtasia*.

search engine   Search engines pretty much drive the internet. The biggest and baddest search engine is that of the Google company. They hire very smart geeky people who do things with mathematical algorithms, whatever *those* are. Anyway, it lets ordinary mortals key in some words (usually at upper right of the screen) and within mere moments . . . there you go, a selection of websites of possible interest is presented to you. This is worth big bucks. Google turns over an eye-bugging twenty billion dollars a year as advertising revenue. You read correctly, B for billions. That's their business. Providing the search tool is really just their way of putting prospective customers in front of advertisers, and they are really good at it.

Not well known is the fact that there are actually hundreds of search engines, not just the few best known like those developed and used by Google, Yahoo, Bing, AltaVista, AOL, Excite, Lycos, HotBot, WebCrawler, Overture, Netscape Search, & Search King. Lots more! Who knew?

shortcuts   A shortcut is a quicker way to open a program than by clicking on **Start**, then **Programs**, then finding the listed program you want. If you have a *desktop icon* for the program, clicking that will take you straight there. The term may also be applied when you perform an action such as clicking and holding down **Ctrl** and hitting the letter **s,** to save your work. [This is quicker than first clicking the pull-down screen, and only then clicking "Save".] Likewise, **Ctrl + b** is the shortcut for **bold** to "bolden"/embold a highlighted word or phrase; and **Ctrl + i** for italicize. To undo those effects you repeat the action.

Skype.com With Skype – it is free to register with them – one can type messages, or use a headset to speak, to anyone else who is registered and whose Skype name you know. In effect, international hour-long "phone" calls can be made free or at very low cost via your computer, one-to-one or as conference calls.

snailmail Snailmail is the jocular but useful word of rhymed syllables which distinguishes light-speed email from the letters delivered by regular mail service in any country. However good the service is, it cannot deliver text like email. But for the foreseeable future, many things will still need to be delivered in physical form.

social networking websites The best known at this time are *Facebook, MySpace* and *Twitter*. In 2006, MySpace, owned by NewsCorp, was the most popular social networking website in the U.S., and in April 2008, Facebook overtook MySpace as the largest such site internationally.

software That's the general word for all the electronic programs which, when they run, we don't actually see happening—just the results as they appear on our screens. Software programs operate in many applications – such as a vehicle's cruise control – where there is no screen involved. In fact, all computer activity needs software, and screens are only for when humans require a visible *interface*.

spam Spam is the name in the email world for multiple unsolicited, unwanted messages. To spam is to send out such mailings. Spamming is the practise of doing so. However, users may find that they actually supplied their email address and permission (for example, "to be notified of further products of interest" or some such wording) to a list which has been passed on to the new sender. Therefore the sender was technically not a spammer, BUT must provide (in the email) a return address and the means to "unsubscribe" forthwith.

spellcheckers have been around for a while as a normal part of word processing. They are sometimes blamed for people "not being able to spell". Actually they can help us to be better natural spellers, and, while good spelling is a useful skill, it's not the be-all and end-all. So, to use a spellchecker well, we should always double check with a human brain – our own. The thing is, the spellchecker really only **alerts us** to a possible problem, whether a simple keystroke-error "typo", or a genuine incorrect spelling (good!) BUT it relies on the human to confirm that the result is the one we want. Set a spellchecker to the English you are working with (U.S., U.K.).

Steam is described as *"a digital distribution ... multiplayer digital distributor of games and related media online, from small independent developers to larger software houses. Steam also has ... automated game updates, and in-game voice and chat functionality. As of 2010, there are over 1,100 games available through Steam. In January 2010 Valve Corporation claimed that it had surpassed 25 million active user accounts. Although Valve never releases sales figures, Steam is estimated to have a 70% share of the digital distribution market for video games."* (from *Wikipedia*)

I guess It will come as no surprise that the game players of Steam's eleven hundred video games seem mostly to be from a young demographic – yet by no means all. The above description gives clues about the way computer-culture is changing our habits, and how far "out of touch" this writer's generation has become. Should we be fazed? Heck no.

Steve Jobs founder of Apple Inc. See the short bio under J.

streaming This is when the computer is downloading information and presenting it to you as it arrives. It's called streaming. That's fine for printed documents. Audiofiles may be received (over the phone line) fast enough so that the human voice is listened to with little delay and therefore the voice is natural-sounding.. Video is the most intensive user of capacity, hence the "streaming" of video transmission may be delayed. You get a stop-and-start slowed-down reception of the video. Here's a case where demand for speed and functionality is outrunning the desire to transfer information.

support ticket If and when you are brave enough to make a purchase online, especially of some downloadable software, or a tuition course of some kind, you may be offered an email link, in case of complaint or enquiry, to a **support ticket**. The vendor probably has an outsourced team of people trained to reply with technical assistance, and empowered if necessary to authorize a refund of your money if you were given a money-back guarantee with your purchase, which is a normal practise.

T

Tag   The word tag seems to have many senses for those computer programmers who know and use geek-speak. Tags, if I have this even halfway right, are examples of "metadata", so that the computer and its human slaves can keep track of processes which are necessary for the computer's operation and *housekeeping*. The *file extensions* which are seen as suffix to file names, like **.exe**, **.pdf, .bmp**, **.gif,** are only one kind of tag, and the name possibly is loosely applied here, because those are correctly called file extensions. As for the deeper meaning of tags, I don't lose sleep over them, and neither should you.

thumbnail   As in, an artist's "thumbnail sketch". The term is used of a small digital image, thumbnail size, big enough so that we can identify the subject of the image, but not using very much of the stored digital data which, when expanded, shows us the whole photograph of the baby in the bath which will embarrass him or her in later life.

tower   Most home computers are contained in a "tower". That is, their important bits and pieces are in the high-rise metal box called a tower.

Remember… the screen we look at is <u>not</u> the computer, though it can give that impression.

Track changes   This is a powerful tool within the MS Word word processor, enabling the writer or writers of a document to keep track of all editing revisions as work progresses, and possibly goes back and forth through several hands. Literally, this software tool is able to track all **changes**. Draft reports and so forth will show the tracked changes, right up until the documentation is deemed ready for the end-reader.

Like much else, when we "drill down" into the detail, we'd see that there is a whole lot of jargon associated with just this one tool, a sub-language to get used to. So too if we were to open out the special terms for page-sizing, or editorial markup language, and headers and footers – or all those exotic font names. That way we'd have a thousand or more entries in this book, and the idea here is to stick to a word list of modest compass.

translation (MT or machine translation) Computer programs for translating from one language to another were once like the holy grail to software designers. In the past forty years such programs have become available with ever improving functionality, but still short of foolproof ability to avoid error, especially in regard to recognizing idiom, or irony and other figurative usage. In other words, simple dictionary meanings are easy for a computer. Idiomatic meanings are tricky. One online service is **Google Translate** which is said to translate between 35 different languages.

Twitter is a website, owned by Twitter Inc., "offering a social networking and micro-blogging service enabling its users to send and read other users' messages called tweets. ... As of late 2009, users can follow lists of authors instead of just following individual authors." (*Wikipedia*)

U

undelete   If you have pressed the **delete** action to remove an email from your *browser*, the word **undelete** now replaces the former word *delete* in the top row of options (where it says things like New Message, *Mark as*, Move to …). The instructions are meant to be intuitive and easily followed. If you want the old email back, just press **undelete**. This brings back (restores) the email, which had been, as it were, parked safely in case you wanted to see it again. Every browser has its different wording and choice of options, but they will allow at least a one-time undelete.

unsubscribe The un- words are fairly numerous but self explanatory. If you have signed up for a course, an email newsletter, a subscription, a membership of any kind, you can be sure that the messages – and any credit card monthly debits you signed for – are likely to keep coming until you successfully "unsubscribe".

unzip   See the entry for *zipfile*.

upload (and **download**)   Most users *download* data a lot more often than they upload. But you may wish to **upload** your very good digital photographs to a site such as **fotolia.com** and make them available for a fee to commercial users who would download selected ones for their needs, paying you a royalty for the privilege. In similar way, if you experiment with self-publishing by going to Amazon's CreateSpace.com, you will be asked, when your material is ready, to **upload a PDF file**. Not hard. Type your text in a normal document and, when done, hit **Save As** – one of the options that comes up is, "Save as a PDF file." Then upload.

URL (say "You-are-ell") This is the fancy name for a web address (http://www . . . etc). It stands for Uniform Resource Locator which doesn't matter in the slightest. People are becoming accustomed to using the initials as a word. "Gimme the URL of your blog. I'll go take a look." *Search engines* have become so convenient and capable that many people hardly know the difference between entering an exact URL address in the *browser*, usually at top left of the screen, and entering a search phrase (for example in *Google* or *Yahoo*) usually at top right. The search then produces a choice of many clickable addresses, in order of likely relevance depending on the search term you typed. See too *active link*.

USB cables *Wikipedia* says this about USB connection – "Universal Serial Bus (USB) is a set of connectivity specifications developed by Intel in collaboration with industry leaders. USB allows high-speed, easy connection of peripherals to a PC."

That's all we need to hear. Emerging back in 1995, USB connections effectively became the standard from 2002 on. None of your older hardware will connect with anything newer than that. This might be annoying. But the convenience of the post-2002 era is worth the changeover, because all your stuff now can connect to your (newer) computer's "ports" with the same kind of plug or socket. The word "bus" just indicates a cabled-together highway of wires for the computer's own internal communication. *Wikipedia* also says: *"When plugged in, everything configures automatically. USB is the most successful interconnect in the history of personal computing and has migrated into consumer electronics (CE) and mobile products."*

V

Valve Corporation are the proprietors of the *Steam* video game platform, said to have around 70% of business traffic for digital downloads of online games, and 25 million users.

video-sharing   This is what so many computer users aspired to – the swapping of video that they themselves had created, or letting friends see clips taken from favorite TV shows and movies (mostly in breach of copyright). Thus was born the giant YouTube.com website. See *YouTube*,

virtual memory   So far as I can tell, virtual memory is a bunch of techniques by which that the geekiest of computer guys manage to fool a computer into thinking it has more memory than it really does. The editor of the *Wikipedia* article comments, "This article may need copy-editing", which is possibly edit-speak for, "I don't understand it either."

virtual reality   "Out upon the seeming!" says a character from Shakespeare. Virtual-anything implies a seeming-to-be-something else. If you lose yourself in a good book, or a movie, you are for the moment "virtually" in the world of the story, in an imagined place which is not the physical one where your body is occupying space. The movie The Matrix uses the premise that humans live in a "virtual world", which seems real to them, while their actual bodies and brains stay obliviously hooked up to computers. Online role-play games take their players one step towards this futuristic scenario.

virus   Computers can get sick too, and one way is when they get infected by a "virus" – not a literal one like a human 'flu virus but a file with spurious but very harmful "instructions" to the computer to do bad things, such as deleting important operational files, or your valuable data. The makers and senders of these malicious programs have some technical smarts, but the ethics of a naughty two year old. Don't open suspicious attachments to emails. Ask about the best anti-virus software as used by people you trust. Reliable anti-virus software, once installed, is updated almost daily without action on your part, as new viral threats are detected and fixed. Note that this book is not a procedure manual!

voice recognition software is becoming available as the required software becomes ever more sophisticated, even for home computers. High-end security software already uses this kind of application, and you may have encountered, over the telephone, utilities or services (cable and satellite TV providers come to mind) where your identity is verified by voice recognition. Whether this is something to celebrate is another matter.

W

wallpaper   The name is evocative, but simply refers to the background pattern or picture on the computer screen. No sticky paste is involved.

Web   The term 'the Web' has become a synonym for the Internet, with or without capital letters; likewise the phrase World-Wide-Web (origin of the **www** still often found in web addresses).

webcam   Not a duck. A webcam's a small digital camera. Sits on top of, or alongside, your screen; came with its easily-loaded software and a *USB* cable to connect it to the back of your computer. It's entirely up to you whether or not you have it switched on, so that other computer users can see you.

Webcrawler – another proprietary *search engine*. It's quite interesting that the name says what search engines **do**. They crawl the web. They do so using mathematically defined robot crawlers (called "bots"). No doubt their moms love them.

web monkey is a not entirely complimentary term in the industry for an amateur creator of websites.

Wikipedia.com   Wikipedia, founded by Jim Wales in 2001, is a not-for-profit online encyclopedia, largely user-written. Information posted may be challenged by others, and citations can be demanded by the managers of the website. Articles may be revised from time to time.

wild card   A question mark (?) search is for a single character, and an asterisk (*) search is for multiple characters. That is, you can use one or the other to replace the unknown part of a phrase when you do a search for a file you have lost track of. At the Start menu you will see the Search utility with its icon in the shape of a magnifying glass.

Windows This is the name for the "graphical interface" developed by the Microsoft company for IBM-clone PCs. It improved upon the older MS-DOS system in emulation of Apple's computers which had led the way in this move to more user-friendly computers of the '80s and '90s.

Wolfdale This entry is only here because I like words with 'wolf' in them. It can't possibly be one you are looking up. Turns out that **Wolfdale** is the name of Apple's most recently discontinued (at time of writing) Core 2 Duo microprocessor in their iMac computer. Bet you didn't know that! Neither did I. Its little buddies (other chips) have names like Clovertown, Harpertown, Merom, and Penryn (which was still current in late 2010). What a strange world the geeky people live in.

Word Microsoft Word, MSWord – or simply Word – is the name by which we know the word processing software normally loaded in every Windows-running PC; also part of the Microsoft Office suite of programs (along with the spreadsheet program called Excel). MSWord is by far the most commonly used word processor.

Wordpress web builder software released in 2003 by Matt Mullenweg. *Wikipedia* has this to say: *"It has many features including a plug-in architecture and a template system. Used by over 12% of the 1,000,000 biggest websites, WordPress is the most popular CMS in use today."* CMS stands for Content Management System.

word processing is ...almost...what we might once simply have called typing. We still type. However, typing on a computer's keyboard is just the main way you "talk" to the computer. Let's say you are typing a letter. We'll call it a *document*, and that avoids confusion with the other meaning of 'letter' in English, a letter of the alphabet. In word-processing you get to choose many things about the way the finished document will look: size, style and color of the alphabetic letters. Each individual letter can be **bold** or *italic* – or both ***italic & bold***. All at the click of your mouse. Any color you want. And in any *font* , from a wide range. You probably would not write a long document like this if it's for a college paper, or your own notes for an easy-to-read presentation. The point is – you have dozens of *fonts* to pick from. So it makes sense to speak of processing words, not merely typing them. Making changes is EASY.

This book is a word-list, and of course is not a manual on the production of documents using word-processing software. You have help near at hand if your computer is already up and running, because the Word program – like many – has its own **Help** facility. You don't need the internet for this. The Help tool is a stand-alone feature on your computer, whenever Word is installed. Open it. Type a question. You should be able to zero in on a useful answer to most questions. Furthermore, Windows (that's the operating system, remember) has its tutorials right there for new users, to view, and to return to, until they feel more comfortable with both the hardware and the software. And if you start out as a two-finger typist, not a problem! Take it easy, and enjoy exploring the experience.

Wordy.com is one online editing service. Clients who want copy (text) checked for correct English have several ways to send their text (doc; docx; txt, pdf) to the Copenhagen-based home-site. Most customers are non-native users of English. Copy to edit can be general, for web-based business, commercial, academic, or in any professional specialty.

WYSIWYG The initials for What You See Is What You Get. Say it as wizzi-wigg. It means that you can type and see on screen the result in plain language, and not in some computer code. The computer actually has to work harder to make this happen. Maybe computers really are smarter than people, and have to talk down to us by putting messages into human language. How annoying.

X Y Z

XMind.com Just one example of the kind of invented word which proliferates on the Web, as in advertising generally. XMind markets chart-drawing software for business planning.

Yahoo! This company went public in March 1995 and has headquarters in California. Its core business is internet operations of various kinds, but the public knows it mainly for *email* access and its *search engine* capability, second only in popularity to that of *Google*.

YouTube It's a huge *video-sharing* website, now hosting many hundreds of millions of videos, typically from one to ten minutes in length, uploaded to YouTube by ordinary individuals as well as by corporate entities. To join is free. Even without registering (joining up) anyone can view most of the videos. Some of the videos are funny and quirky, some informative, some promoting products or causes. Some videos are available only to registered viewers over 18 years.

There are other video-posting websites (one such is Hulu) but YouTube.com – first activated in February 2005, and founded by three ex-staff from *PayPal* – grew so fast that it was bought by Google in November 2006 for 1.65 billion dollars.

Since 2009 YouTube markets full-length movies via its web presence, and in 2010 added streaming of international sports events. As at mid-2010, YouTube was considered to be the world's third biggest internet site, after Google and Facebook.

zipfile   This file format has been around since 1989, and is for data compressing and archiving. A zip file contains one or more files compressed to reduce file size. The process helps your computer deal more efficiently with downloads and its store of data. All <u>we</u> need to know is that our computer has "built-in zip support …under the name 'compressed folders'" as the Wikipedia article puts it. You should not really need to buy third-party software for zipping (compressing) and unzipping files.

notes and additions

aHansel^imprint

Manufactured by Amazon.ca
Bolton, ON